Come 'union' cation

20 Common Marriage Problems

A Guide & Workbook for Christian Spouses

About Us

MARRIED AS ONE LLC
Come 'union' cation

Married As One LLC is a Christian ministry offering a unique approach to marriage coaching. They offer marriage coaching that includes spoken word poetry, photography, costume design, and praise-filled worship workshops to strengthen marriages and relationships.

Led by Felice and Retta Mathieu(in the picture above), they provide practical biblical advice aimed at empowering spouses to overcome common marriage problems. Retta combines her church upbringing (being a pastor's daughter) with her photography and design skills to create unique and authentic images. Together, Felice and Retta are committed to excellence and helping couples build strong, healthy relationships. Choose Married As One LLC for a comprehensive approach to relationship building.

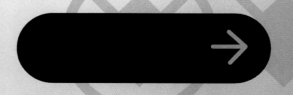

Visit Our Website
www.marriedasone.com

Services

"Marriage is a major vehicle for the gospel's remaking of your heart from the inside out and your life from the ground up."
_Pastor Tim Keller

Pre-Marriage Coaching

Equip yourself for a successful marriage by mastering the skills to overcome the inevitable challenges that arise in every relationship.

Marriage Tune-ups

Just like a car, your marriage requires regular tune-ups to keep it running smoothly. Our Christian marriage sessions are here to provide the tools and support you need to keep your marriage 'running' like Jesus designed .

Marriage Workshops

Looking to strengthen your marriage and deepen your connection with your spouse? Join our Christian marriage workshop and learn practical skills and biblical principles for a healthy and thriving relationship.

- **FREE** Christian Marriage Books
- Professional Photography
- Spoken Word Performances
- Praise and Worship Service
- Prayer and Fellowship

MEET US
704-312-2266
@marriedasone
felice@marriedasone.com

Services

Pre-Marriage Coaching

Equip yourself for a successful marriage by mastering the skills to overcome the inevitable challenges that arise in every relationship.

Marriage Tune-ups

Just like a car, your marriage requires regular tune-ups to keep it running smoothly. Our Christian marriage sessions are here to provide the tools and support you need to keep your marriage 'running' like Jesus designed .

Marriage Workshops

Looking to strengthen your marriage and deepen your connection with your spouse? Join our Christian marriage workshop and learn practical skills and biblical principles for a healthy and thriving relationship.

- **FREE** Christian Marriage Books
- Professional Photography
- Spoken Word Performances
- Praise and Worship Service
- Prayer and Fellowship

MEET US
704-312-2266
@marriedasone
felice@marriedasone.com

20 Most Common
Marriage Problems and Solutions

TABLE OF CONTENTS

Introduction

-Metaphor

"When you take your car to a repair shop, they connect it to a special machine that performs a diagnostic check on your vehicle. The machine generates 'codes' that describe any potential problems. Similarly, the Bible serves as the "special machine" in this metaphor, and Jesus is the 'mechanic', with perfect teachings still relevant for today.

To improve our marriage, we(spouses) should hold ourselves accountable and draw inspiration from our personal relationship with Jesus. By addressing the sins that manifest themselves through our marital problems, we can be sanctified by the Holy Spirit and positively transform our marriages. We believe that if each spouse focuses on removing the "log" from their own eye instead of blaming each other, the Holy Spirit's sanctifying power will divinely transform marriages for His glory."

Introduction

This book provides principle-based guidance rather than a step-by-step guide. Keep these *five principles* in mind:
- Pray to the Holy Spirit for truth.
- Use these exercises for self-accountability.
- Work on each flaw individually and gradually, rather than all at once.
- Ask loved ones to be your "mirror" for identifying character blind spots that offer growth opportunities.
- Find ways to have *fun* with this.

Each section will contain a bible verse, for context.
Each section will contain a statement for explanation.
Each section will include reflective question(s).
In the fill in the blanks, be honest with the answers.
Spouses can do the sections together or separately and discuss the results.

Awareness

Awareness is a crucial aspect of changed behavior because it is the first step towards recognizing the need for change. When individuals become aware of their behavior and the impact it has on themselves and others, they are more likely to take responsibility for their actions and make a conscious effort to change. In this way,"we consider awareness a potent tool for our Holy Spirit."

"Do nothing from selfishness or empty conceit, but with humility of mind regard one another as more important than yourselves; do not merely look out for your own personal interests, but also for the interests of others."
Philippians 2:3-5

Let's explore how prioritizing our individual wants, needs and feelings over the needs of our marriage can have harmful effects. Selfishness has a way of making our spouse feel like their needs are less important than ours.

What are 3 areas in your marriage that you believe go more your way, than *your* (you and your spouse) ways?

_____

_____

_____

_____

_____

_____

_____

_____

_____

_____

_____

02   PRIDE

 "For all that is in the world—the desires of the flesh and the desires of the eyes and pride in possessions—is not from the Father but is from the world."

1 John 2:16

Pride can divide a marriage by causing a lack of accountability, arrogance, and a refusal to apologize. To build a healthy marriage, it's important to prioritize humility over pride, which leads to a deeper connection and mutual respect.

What notable accomplishments have stirred feelings of deep pride and fulfillment? Is it possible that such moments of excessive pride may have contributed to less-than-pleasant patterns of behavior or speech?"

_____

_____

_____

_____

_____

_____

_____

_____

_____

03 **UNFORGIVENESS**

> *"And whenever you stand praying, forgive, if you have anything against anyone, so that your Father also who is in heaven may forgive you your trespasses."*

Mark 11:25

"Perfection is unattainable in this earthly life, and marriages are not sustained by the absence of imperfections, but rather by spouses who possess the divine capacity to forgive, as we are forgiven each day.

What areas in your heart might still require forgiveness for your spouse?

_____

_____

_____

_____

_____

_____

_____

_____

_____

_____

_____

_____

04 NEGATIVITY

" *"Therefore do not be anxious about tomorrow, for tomorrow will be anxious for itself. Sufficient for the day is its own trouble."*

Matthew 6:34

Life is full of unpredictability, and unfortunate circumstances that may befall us regardless of our efforts. Nonetheless, we have the power to cultivate a positive attitude that radiates joy and makes us a delight to be around.

How can we enhance our positivity to become a more pleasant presence in the lives of our spouses?

_____

_____

_____

_____

_____

_____

_____

_____

_____

_____

_____

"Teach me your way, O Lord, that I may walk in your truth; unite my heart to fear your name."

Psalm 86:11

Sometimes when we make mistakes, we don't want to admit it because we feel embarrassed or less than. But when we do this, it can be hard to get better and do things differently. To make progress and become the best who Christ desires us to be, we need to prayerfully be honest with ourselves.

What faults and flaws have others pointed out to you, but you have denied, that may be worth reflecting on?

_____

_____

_____

_____

_____

_____

_____

_____

_____

_____

06 INSECURITY

"The thief comes only to steal and kill and destroy. I came that they may have life and have it abundantly."

John 10:10

Insecurities are an inescapable part of the human experience, and while one's significant other can offer support in addressing them, the responsibility for managing them ultimately falls upon the individual.

Reflecting on this, have any of your own insecurities placed undue strain on your spouse?

_____

_____

_____

_____

_____

_____

_____

_____

_____

_____

_____

> 66 *"Whoever loves discipline loves knowledge, but he who hates reproof is stupid."*
>
> **Proverbs 12:11**

Defensiveness can be harmful to a marriage as it often creates a cycle of blame and resentment between spouses. When one partner becomes defensive, it can make the other partner feel unheard or dismissed, leading to further tension and frustration.

How can you break the cycle of defensiveness and learn to communicate in a more constructive and empathetic way?

_____

_____

_____

_____

_____

_____

_____

_____

_____

_____

> 66 *"Stop depriving one another, except by agreement for a time, so that you may devote yourselves to prayer, and come together again so that Satan will not tempt you because of your lack of self-control."*
>
> **1 Corinthians 7:5**

Unfaithfulness can be devastating to a marriage, causing deep emotional pain and eroding trust between spouses. It can lead to feelings of betrayal, anger, and resentment, and may ultimately lead to the breakdown of the relationship.

How can you personally work to rebuild trust and heal from the emotional wounds caused by infidelity? What specific steps can you take to prevent it from happening in the future?

_____

_____

_____

_____

_____

_____

_____

_____

_____

_____

> " *"Would not God discover this? For he knows the secrets of the heart."*
>
> **Psalm 44:21**

Keeping secrets in a marriage is like hiding important information from your best friend. When we keep secrets, we make our loved ones feel sad and worried, and it can be hard for them to trust us. This can make it difficult for both partners to talk about their feelings and solve problems together. To build a strong and healthy marriage, it's important to be honest and share our thoughts and feelings with each other.

"What secrets do you think are unacceptable to keep from your spouse, and are you committed to being just as open and honest with them?"

_____

_____

_____

_____

_____

_____

_____

_____

10

LIES

Lies can be incredibly damaging to a marriage, eroding trust and making it difficult for partners to communicate and build a strong emotional connection. When one partner lies, it can lead to feelings of betrayal and resentment, and may ultimately cause the breakdown of the relationship.

What commitments can you make to prevent lies from being the norm in your relationship?

_____

_____

_____

_____

_____

_____

_____

_____

_____

_____

_____

SEX

> ❝ *"How beautiful you are and how pleasing, my love, with your delights! Your stature is like that of the palm, and your breasts like clusters of fruit."*
>
> **Song of Solo mon7:6**

Lack of sexual intimacy in a marriage can lead to a range of negative consequences, including feelings of frustration, rejection, and disconnection between partners. Over time, this can create a rift between spouses and make it difficult for them to maintain a close emotional bond.

How can you address a lack of sexual intimacy in your marriage and find ways to reconnect and build a healthy and fulfilling sex life together?

_____

_____

_____

_____

_____

_____

_____

_____

_____

_____

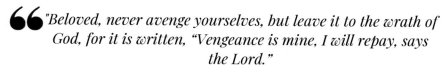

"Beloved, never avenge yourselves, but leave it to the wrath of God, for it is written, "Vengeance is mine, I will repay, says the Lord."

Romans 12:19

Revenge can lead to feelings of bitterness and resentment, making it difficult for spouses to trust each other and communicate effectively. To build a strong and healthy Christian marriage, it's important for couples to prioritize forgiveness and work through their conflicts in a way that honors their commitment to God and each other.

How can you draw on your faith and the teachings of Christ to cultivate a spirit of forgiveness and avoid the pitfalls of revenge in their marriage?

_____

_____

_____

_____

_____

_____

_____

_____

_____

_____

_____

13 LACK OF ATTENTION

"Husbands, love your wives, as Christ loved the church and gave himself up for her," Ephesians."

Romans 12:19

As spouses, we need to recognize the dangers of neglecting each other in our marriage. It's like a plant that slowly withers away without water. When we fail to give each other the attention, time, and care we need, it can create distance and disconnection. We need to prioritize our relationship and find ways to give each other the attention we need to thrive and grow together.

What principles should we commit to, so that we avoid the danger of neglect and build a strong and healthy marriage that will stand the test of time?

_____

_____

_____

_____

_____

_____

_____

_____

_____

_____

14 LACK OF INVESTMENT

 "The point is this: whoever sows sparingly will also reap sparingly, and whoever sows bountifully will also reap bountifully."

2 Corinthians 9:6

Lack of investment in a marriage can lead to its downfall. It's like a bank account that slowly gets depleted without any deposits. We need to consistently invest time, energy, and effort into our relationship to keep it strong and healthy.

What commitments can we make to each other, daily, to invest in our marriage and ensure a bright future together?

_____

_____

_____

_____

_____

_____

_____

_____

_____

_____

_____

_____

"So they are no longer two but one flesh. What therefore God has joined together, let not man separate."

Matthew 19:6

The lack of support in a marriage can cause deep emotional pain and feelings of isolation. When we don't feel supported by our spouse, we may begin to doubt ourselves and our ability to overcome challenges.

How can we better support each other in our marriage and create a stronger bond of love and trust?

_____

_____

_____

_____

_____

_____

_____

_____

_____

_____

16 LACK OF SELF-IMPROVEMENT

> 66 *"For all have sinned and fall short of the glory of God."*
> **Romans 3:23**

"When we stop growing and learning, our marriage can start to turn and burn. For love is not static, it needs to flow, and self-improvement helps it to grow."

How will you transcend the shallow pursuits of self-improvement and commit to a deep, meaningful transformation for the sake of your beloved spouse?

_____

_____

_____

_____

_____

_____

_____

_____

_____

_____

_____

_____

_____

17 LACK OF EMPATHY

> " *Be kind to one another, tenderhearted, forgiving one another, as God in Christ forgave you.* "
>
> **Ephesians 4:32**

Without empathy, it becomes difficult to truly understand and support your partner's emotions and needs, which can create a toxic cycle of miscommunication and hurt.

What can we consistently do to cultivate greater empathy and emotional connection in our marriage?

_____

_____

_____

_____

_____

_____

_____

_____

_____

_____

_____

_____

18 LACK OF KNOWLEDGE

> *"If any of you lacks wisdom, let him ask God, who gives generously to all without reproach, and it will be given him."*
>
> **James 1:5**

Lack of knowledge in marriage might pose a serious risk to the union. It could result in misunderstandings, poor communication, and irrational hopes. Couples that lack information may find it difficult to communicate and meet one another's needs, which can cause anger and animosity.

Are you actively and consistently exploring new resources that can bring transformation to your marriage?

_____

_____

_____

_____

_____

_____

_____

_____

_____

_____

_____

19 SILENCE

> 66 *"Even a fool who keeps silent is considered wise; when he closes his lips, he is deemed intelligent."*
>
> **Proverbs 17:28**

Silence in a marriage can be dangerous as it creates an emotional distance between spouses. It can lead to a lack of communication and understanding, which can lead to feelings of loneliness and isolation. Unresolved issues and resentment can build up over time, causing irreparable damage to the relationship. Couples must strive to break the silence and communicate with each other openly and honestly to maintain a healthy and strong marriage.

How can spouses create a safe space to encourage open communication in their marriage?

_____

_____

_____

_____

_____

_____

_____

_____

_____

"Let no corrupting talk come out of your mouths, but only such as is good for building up, as fits the occasion, that it may give grace to those who hear."

Ephesians 4:29

When one partner in a marriage treats the other with disrespect, it can cause hurt, anger, and resentment. It may weaken spouses' trust in one another and hurt feelings, making it hard for them to cooperate and talk to one another. The emotional and mental health of both partners may suffer as a result of the poisonous environment created. It can cause marital strife in the long run.

How have your loved ones pointed out behaviors you have that may be perceived as disrespectful?

_____

_____

_____

_____

_____

_____

_____

_____

_____

It is our prayers that this resource aids marriages, biblically and effectively, worldwide. Donations to our nonprofit make that possible. Consider passing it forward. Our nonprofit's mission is to help "whole families stay whole."

Ways to donate:

- Marriagesharing.org
- Cashapp:Marriage Sharing
- **Text** To Give: **704-313-1885**

Made in the USA
Middletown, DE
30 September 2023

39530977R00018